BEN FOLDS FIVE

THE SOUND OF THE LIFE OF THE MIND

Photography by Tom Freitag

ISBN 978-1-4768-7466-1

HAL•LEONARD®
CORPORATION
7777 W. BLUEMOUND RD. P.O. BOX 13819 MILWAUKEE, WI 53213

Visit Hal Leonard Online at
www.halleonard.com

CONTENTS

Erase Me

Words and Music by Ben Folds

Double time ($\quarternote$ = 72)

Downstems: Bass cues

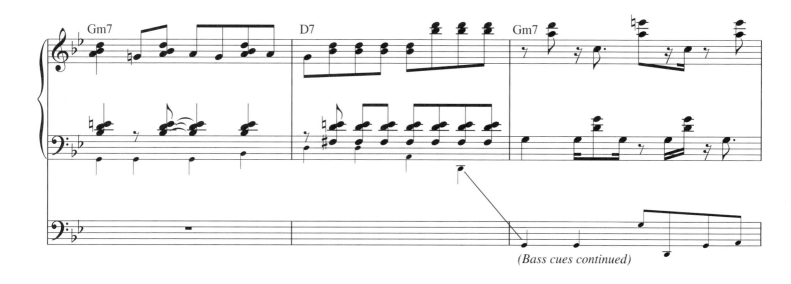

(Bass cues continued)

Michael Praytor, Five Years Later

Words and Music by Ben Folds

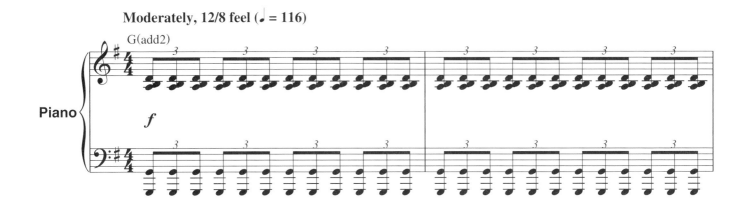

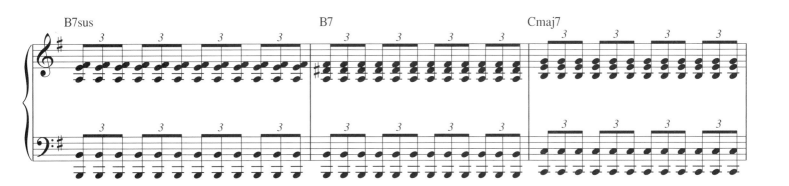

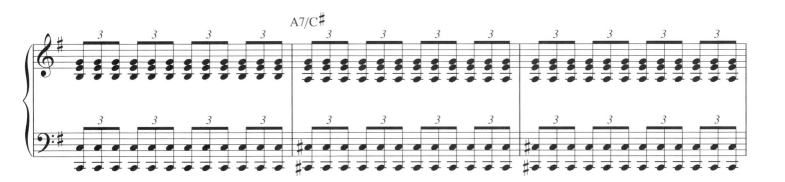

dis - ap - pear in - to the sky.

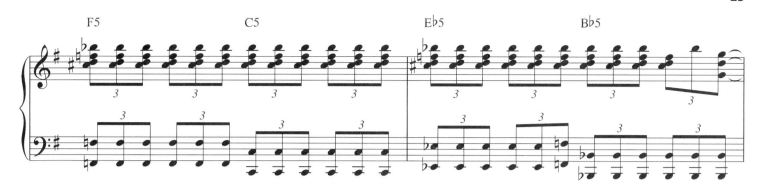

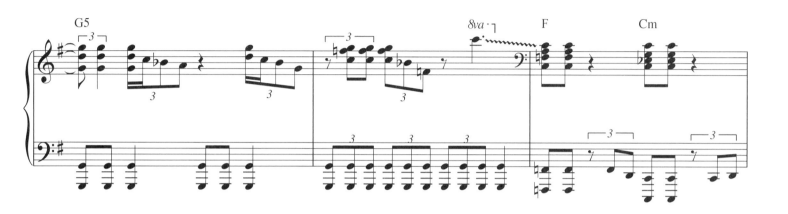

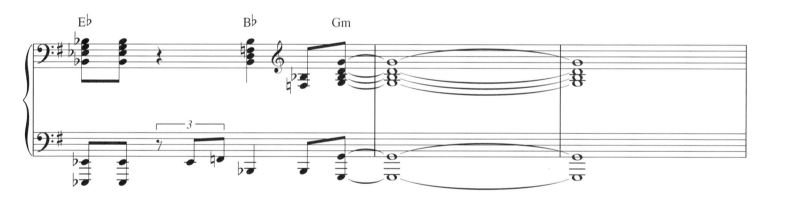

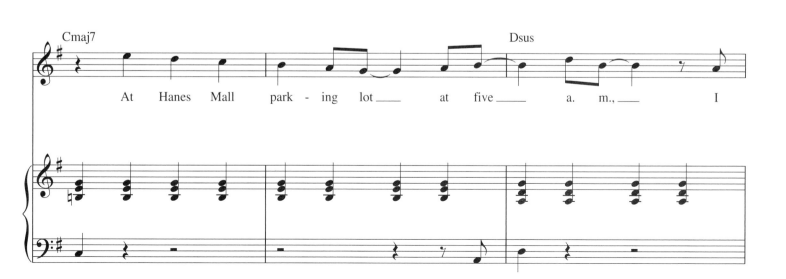

At Hanes Mall park - ing lot ___ at five ___ a. m., ___ I

Guess I'll see you a - round." Guess I'll see you a - round.

Mi - chael Pray - tor.

Mi - chael Pray - tor.

Sky High

Words and Music by Darren Jessee

Shat-tered at dawn, ___ so far for so long, feel-ing ___ new - ly

an' all ___ the blue ___ sky.

Ah, _____ sky ___ high.

The Sound Of The Life Of The Mind

Words by Nick Hornby
Music by Ben Folds

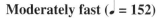

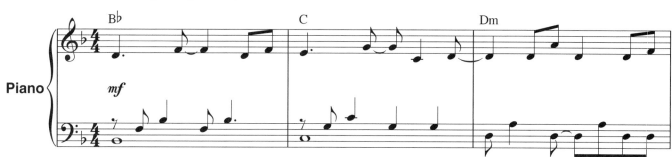

It rocks like a moth - er. _____

(Oh, _____ (Oh.) _ (Oh, _____ oh, _ oh.) _____
oh, _ oh, _

oh, _ (Oh.) _ oh.) _____ She's

cut 'em all out of her so - cial cir - cle,

On Being Frank

Words and Music by Ben Folds

Draw A Crowd

Words and Music by Ben Folds

Chords in parentheses are played as ghost notes.

Fender Rhodes tacet to end

Synth bass cues

66

(Piano L.H. as recorded)

Do It Anyway

Words and Music by Ben Folds

said   I'd   nev - er   say; _____

read   me   off   a   list   of   the   things   I

used   to   not   like,   but   now   I   think   are

o - kay.

Some - times it's not sub - jec - tive, wrong and __ right.

Deep down __ you know it's down - right wrong, but

you're in - vin - ci - ble _____ to - night, _____ so you

do it an - y - way.

Spoken: It's done;

You did it.

De - spite your grand at - tempts, the

chips are set to fall, and all the sto - ries you

might weave _____ can not _____ ne - go - ti - ate _____ them all. _____

Do it an - y - way.

Be hon - est, an - y -

way.

So tell me what I said I'd never do; tell me what I've said I'd never say; read me off a

list of the things that I used to not

like, but now I think are o-

kay, yeah, yeah, yeah, yeah,

whoa,   whoa, —   whoa, —   whoa.

Downstems: Bass cues

It's gon - na be so ___ ver - y hard ___ to say ___ and watch the

(Do it an - y - way.) (Do it an - y - way.)

(Do it an - y - way.) (Do it an - y - way.)

Hold That Thought

Words and Music by Ben Folds

on a sim - ple, eas - y _____ chart.

Lat - er on ___ that eve - ning on the beach __

___ in San - ta Mon - i - ca, it was a

ver - y risk - y _____ start. __ Sup -

Away When You Were Here

Words and Music by Ben Folds

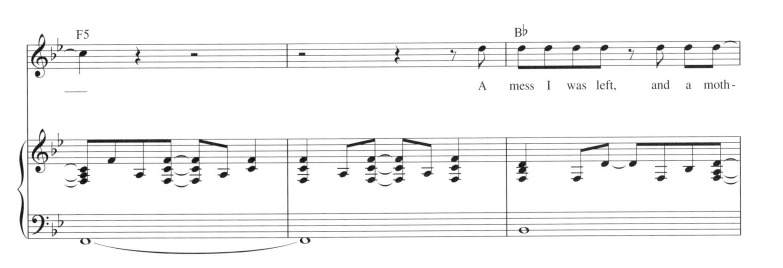

what — I do — with — it all. — And — I've

known ev - 'ry way — you've let —

me down. —

Bass clef notes: Bass cues

Thank You For Breaking My Heart

Words and Music by Ben Folds

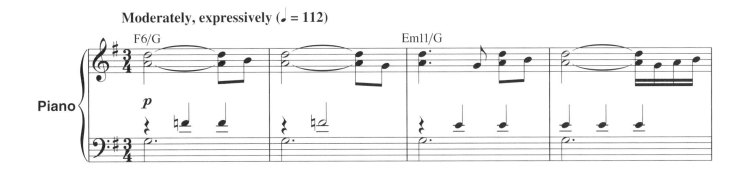

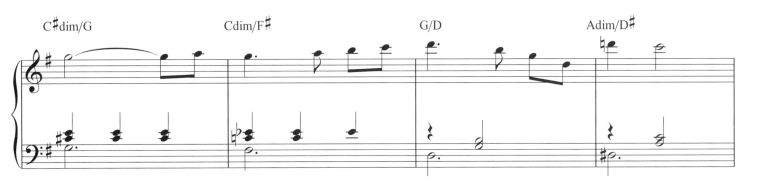

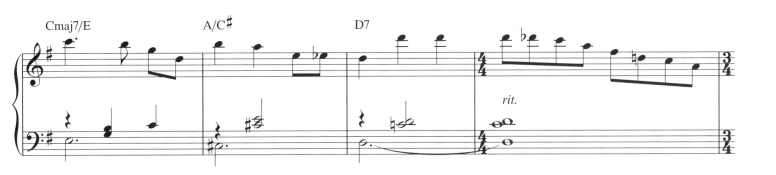

left it wide o - pen and asked you to stay, but

you know bet - ter.

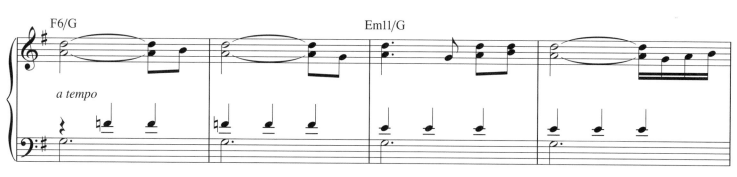

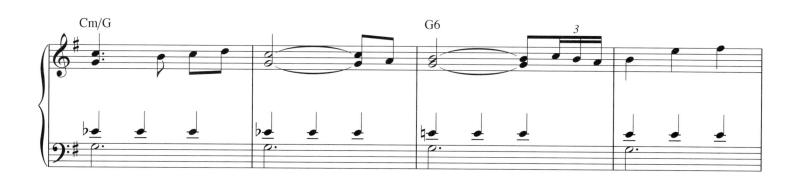

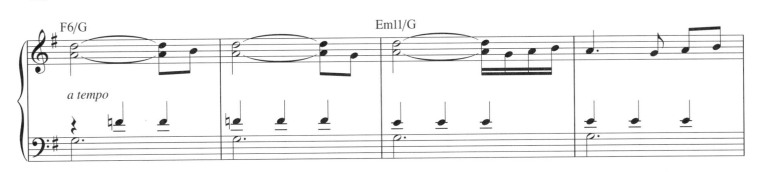

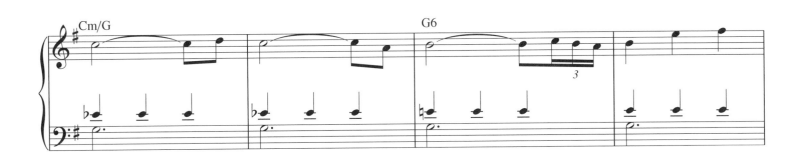

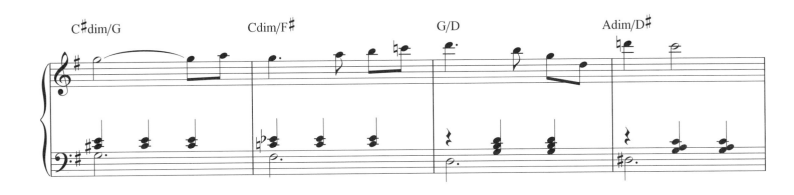

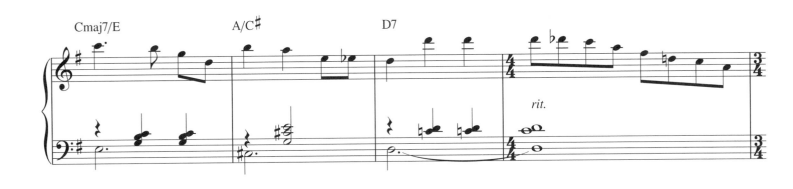